FACT FINDERS

Educational adviser: Arthur Razzell

Ballet

Robin May

Editorial adviser: Mary Clarke

Illustrated by Jeff Burn, Dan Escott,
Ron Hayward and Sean Rudman
Designed by Faulkner/Marks Partnership

Macmillan Education Limited

Adapted and published in
the United States by
Silver Burdett Company,
Morristown, N.J.
1980 Printing

ISBN 0-382-06443-7

Library of Congress
Catalog Card No. 80-50425

Ballet

The Magical World of Ballet

Ballet is a beautiful and exciting type of dance. It takes years to become a ballet dancer.

Dancers practise for hours each day. They start learning ballet when they are very young. The children on the right are rehearsing *The Nutcracker* with Rudolf Nureyev and Merle Park.

Many ballets tell a story. The stories can happen in a palace, a forest, or anywhere. Some ballets have no story. They are just made up of lovely dance movements.

The Rite of Spring (above) is a modern ballet. *The Sleeping Beauty* (right) is an old favourite. You can see the *corps de ballet* in *Swan Lake* in the picture on the left.

Ballet School

Here you can see young dancers at work. Some may be stars one day. Others will join a group called the *'corps de ballet.'*

They all practise every single day at the *barre*. The *barre* is the wooden bar that goes right round the wall of the practice room.

Barre

Holding the *barre* helps a dancer to balance properly when doing special exercises. Teachers watch each movement their pupils make. They watch the stars practising too, and make corrections! Older girls learn to dance on 'pointe' on the tips of their toes (left).

Pointe

Making a Ballet

One of the most important people in ballet is the choreographer. He or she decides which steps the dancers dance. The choreographer also teaches the dancers the steps.

The most famous British choreographer is Frederick Ashton. He is rehearsing dancers on the left.

In ballet you can 'speak' by using signs. This is 'ask'.

This means 'see'. This sign language is called mime.

Standing between the chairs (right) is Ninette de Valois. She was a dancer before she became a famous choreographer. With her are two dancers. Their names are Merle Park and David Wall.

Ninette de Valois is best known as the founder of Britain's Royal Ballet.

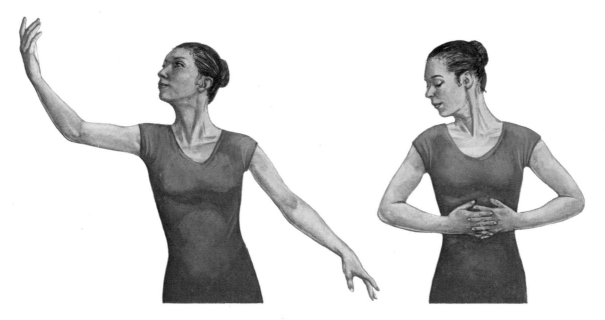

Here the dancer is calling to someone.

This means 'love'. The dancer holds her heart.

Costumes in ballet must look good and be easy to dance in as well.
They have to be carefully fitted.

The dancer making-up her face is Lynn Seymour. Dancers put on a lot of make-up. This is so their faces can be seen clearly in big theatres.

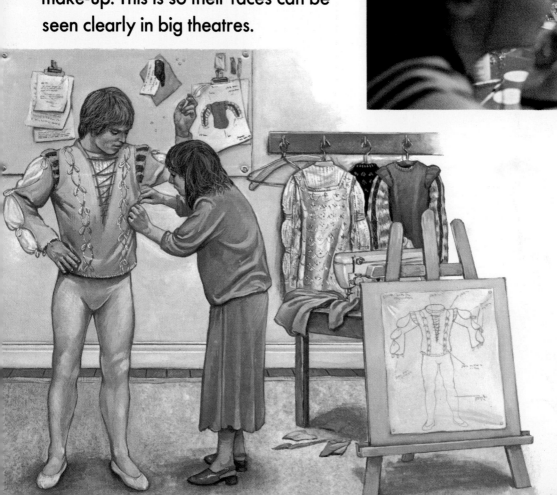

You can see people hard at work in the picture below. Some are moving scenery. Some are making and painting it.

The small picture is a plan of the scene that the audience will see. It is drawn by an artist called a designer.

Plan

How Ballet Began

Ballet began in France about 300 years ago, at the court of King Louis XIV. That is why most ballet words are French.

You can see what an early ballet looked like on the right. The king and his courtiers took part in these ballets. Later, ballets became too hard for ordinary dancers to perform.

A court ballet (above)

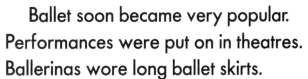

Ballet soon became very popular. Performances were put on in theatres. Ballerinas wore long ballet skirts.

By about 100 years ago, most ballets had become rather unreal. Girls even danced men's parts. Things were different in Russia. Great ballets like *Swan Lake* and *The Nutcracker* were danced there.

Les Sylphides (below)

The Nutcracker

Ballet Reborn

About 70 years ago, ballet in the West was saved by a Russian named Diaghilev. He collected wonderful dancers, artists and musicians together. They created several great ballets which excited people all over Europe.

Diaghilev's first choreographer was called Fokine. This exciting scene shows his *Petrouchka*.

Petrouchka (below)

Romeo and Juliet

Petrouchka is a puppet who has his heart broken. The part was first danced by a dancer called Nijinsky.

Graduation Ball (left) is a lively ballet. *Romeo and Juliet* (far left) is a sad love story.

Graduation Ball (above)

Modern Ballet

All over the world ballet companies are dancing new ballets. These ballets often look very different from classical ballets. Sometimes the dancers even dance in bare feet.

Pierrot Lunaire (above) is danced by the Ballet Rambert. The London Contemporary Dance Theatre Company (right) only do modern ballets.

This modern American ballet called *Rodeo* is about cowboys.

There are some ballets that everyone loves. The most popular is *Swan Lake*. Our pictures show three other favourites. *Romeo and Juliet* (below) has the same story as the play by Shakespeare. Parts of it, like this fight scene, are very exciting. In the end the lovers die.

La Fille Mal Gardée (right) is a love story which is great fun. The name of the ballet means 'the badly guarded girl'.

Above is a scene from *Coppelia*.
She is a doll who seems to come to life.
You can see her and also her maker,
Doctor Coppelius.

Some Superstars

All ballet lovers enjoy watching superstars dance. They are the most exciting dancers in the world.

The female stars in a company are called ballerinas. They dance the most important roles for girls. Below are Anthony Dowell and Lynn Seymour. He is English, she is Canadian.

Many people think that Natalia Makarova (above) is the best ballerina in the world. Here she is dancing in *Swan Lake*. She is Russian but she dances all over the world.

Margot Fonteyn and Rudolf Nureyev were partners for many exciting years. You can see them in *The Sleeping Beauty* on the left.

Glossary

Ballerina   A female ballet dancer. She may dance leading roles in ballets.

Ballet music   Sometimes a ballet is designed to fit music which has already been written. At other times music is specially written for a new ballet.

Barre   The wooden bar that runs round the walls of a ballet practise room. Dancers hold it for exercises. The *barre* helps the dancers to balance.

Choreographer   The person who decides on the steps of a new ballet. He or she teaches the dancers to dance the steps.

Classical ballet   This is a special kind of dancing which can only be done by people who have had ballet training. The words are also used to describe ballets like *Swan Lake* and *The Sleeping Beauty* which have lasted for nearly 100 years.

Corps de ballet   The dancers who dance together but do not take solo parts. The swans in *Swan Lake* are the *corps de ballet*.

Designer   The person who thinks up the scenery and costumes for a new ballet.

Mime   Mime is a sort of sign language. Dancers do not speak, they use their faces, arms and bodies to tell the story instead.

Pointe   A French word meaning tiptoe. A dancer who dances on the tip of her toes is dancing on 'pointe'.

Photo credits: Zoë Dominic; Reg Wilson.
The photographs on pages 6-7 were taken with the kind co-operation of the Arts Educational School, London.